BREAKAWAY

BREAKAWAY

Al Janssen

BUILD
DISCIPLESHIP LEADERSHIP
SEND
EVANGELISM
WIN

1574

**Here's Life
Publishers**

P.O. Box 1576, San Bernardino, CA 92402

BREAKAWAY
by Al Janssen

Published by
HERE'S LIFE PUBLISHERS, INC.
P.O. Box 1576
San Bernardino, CA 92402

HLP Product No. 951087

PRINTED IN THE UNITED STATES OF AMERICA.
Library of Congress Cataloging in Publication Data

Janssen, Al.
  Breakaway.

  1. Hockey players—Biography.   2. Sports—Religious aspects—
Christianity.   I. Title.
GV848.5.A1J36   1985   796.96'2'0922 [B]   85-8676
ISBN 0-89840-082-1 (pbk.)

FOR MORE INFORMATION, WRITE:

L.I.F.E. — P.O. Box A399, Sydney South 2000, Australia
Campus Crusade for Christ of Canada — Box 300, Vancouver, B.C., V6C 2X3, Canada
Campus Crusade for Christ — 103 Friar Street, Reading RG1 1EP, Berkshire, England
Lay Institute for Evangelism — P.O. Box 8786, Auckland 3, New Zealand
Great Commission Movement of Nigeria — P.O. Box 500, Jos, Plateau State Nigeria, West Africa
Life Ministry — P.O. Box/Bus 91015, Auckland Park 2006, Republic of South Africa
Campus Crusade for Christ International — Arrowhead Springs, San Bernardino, CA 92414, U.S.A.

To the players and their families who have been Christian ambassadors in hockey.

Contents

Introduction

It's the most dramatic play in hockey. A player steals the puck, skates past the defensemen and finds himself one-on-one with the goalie. It's a breakaway, that exciting moment when a lone player and the opposing goalie pit their skills against each other in a lightning-quick confrontation.

The players you are about to meet all have experienced their share of breakaways on the ice. They know the thrill of winning the Stanley Cup championship. They've won scoring titles, set records, and earned most valuable player awards. They are among the world's finest hockey players, that elite corps of men who make up the National Hockey League.

But the men in this book are more than just hockey players. They want you to see them on the ice — and in the locker room. They also would like to sit down with you and have a good talk. They would like you to see them in their homes and on the road, away from the crowds and the autograph-seeking fans, so they might tell you the secret to a fulfilling life.

Each of these NHL players has experienced a personal breakaway — a moment when he broke away from his past and entered into a new dimension of life, a spiritual dimension.

That spiritual element has enabled these men to cope with serious injury and overcome alcohol abuse.

It has deepened their family relationships. It has given them added motivation to succeed in their sport. And it provides a purpose for living that will last long after they have played their final NHL game.

So I invite you to sit back, relax, and enjoy a visit with some of North America's most interesting athletes. And in the process, you may find that you will experience your own spiritual breakaway.

—Al Janssen

Ryan Walter

---------------- 1 ----------------

RYAN WALTER

The locker room was quiet as the Montreal Canadiens waited to take the ice. In one corner, centerman Ryan Walter made his final mental preparations, realizing the significance of this contest. The Canadiens were in first place, but by only two points, and they hadn't won in their last six games. Their opponents were the second-place Buffalo Sabres, undefeated in nine games.

But tonight meant even more than a battle for first place, as this was the celebration of the Canadiens' 75th anniversary and the 60th anniversary of the Forum. Though still in the locker room, Ryan could hear the crowd of more than seventeen thousand greeting Canada's prime minister, Brian Mulroney, and his wife, Mila.

On this special night, the Canadiens were wearing
their red jerseys rather than the traditional home white.
Their sweater logo — a large *C* inset with the letter *H*,
signifying "Club de Hockey Canadien" — had remained
unchanged for the last sixty-five years of the team's
storied history. Ryan glanced up at pictures of men who
had made this a symbol of excellence: "Boom Boom"
Geoffrion, Jean Béliveau, Henri Richard, Georges
Vezina and thirty-seven other greats who made up the
Montreal Canadiens' Hall of Fame. Above their portraits
were the words: "To you from failing hands we throw
the torch, be yours to hold it high." The message was
clear: Ryan and his teammates were expected to uphold
the tradition of the Montreal Canadiens and their twenty-
two Stanley Cup championships.

Ryan reviewed his responsibilities. Coach Jacques
Lemaire wanted his line to put pressure on the Sabres'
fine defense, led by their hot-handed goalie, Tom
Barrasso. He mentally reminded himself of an obvious
point: He could not score unless he took some shots.
Then he spent a few moments visualizing his probable
opponent on faceoffs, Brent Peterson, one of the best
in the league. If Ryan didn't win the first couple of
draws, he would switch to his forehand and attempt to
tie up Peterson, hoping a teammate could pick up the
loose puck.

Finally, the coach clapped his hands: "Let's go." The
crowd roared as goalie Steve Penney led the team onto
the ice. Then, after a brief skate, the two teams waited
for the dramatic announcement of the Canadiens'

all-time all-star team. Claude Mouton, Montreal's director of public relations, stood at a plexiglass podium and in dramatic fashion recalled each member's greatness.

Toe Blake, player for thirteen seasons, coach for another thirteen; winner of three Stanley Cups as a player and eight more as a coach, including an unprecedented five straight . . . The crowd gave the all-time coach a standing ovation as he was escorted to center ice on a red carpet.

The noise increased as each star's credentials were recited and the player skated onto the ice in full uniform to take a ceremonial shot on goal. Goalie Jacques Plante, six-time winner of the Vezina Trophy; Doug Harvey, nine times a first-team all-star defenseman; Larry Robinson, the only active member of the Canadiens on the all-time team; Dickie Moore, two-time NHL scoring champion; Jean Béliveau, a center on ten Stanley Cup championship teams; Maurice "Rocket" Richard, first player to score fifty goals in fifty games and a French Canadian who still inflames the passions of Montreal fans thirty years after his NHL suspension instigated a riot in this Forum.

For many fans, the ceremony brought tears, but for Ryan Walter and the present Canadiens, the challenge of upholding the torch would require a level-headed intensity. Half an hour later than normal, the game finally got underway with all the energy of a playoff contest. Six minutes into the first period, Mario Tremblay tipped in

When playing with the Washington Capitols, Ryan Walter was
the youngest team captain selected in the NHL.

a blast by Robinson. Buffalo tied the game seven minutes later. From then on, it was a battle of defenses with fierce checking at both ends of the ice.

Jennifer Walter anxiously watched from her seat seven rows from the ice. As the third period concluded and the teams entered overtime, she admitted it was almost too hard to watch her husband take the crucial faceoffs. She prayed he wouldn't make a mistake that would cost the game.

Earlier in the season, Jennifer had watched on television as Ryan was knocked unconscious during a game at Pittsburgh. "I was really calm," she said during a break in the action. "I immediately started praying and God gave me a peace. Then Ryan called me from the hospital . . . and he kept repeating himself. That's when I really started to pray."

She paused as Ryan took a faceoff to the left of goalie Steve Penney. He won the draw, allowing the defense to push the puck out of trouble. "I don't dare worry about him getting hurt, or I'd be a nervous wreck every game."

The game ended in a tie, but the mood was upbeat in the Canadiens' locker room. They had played well, especially on defense in limiting Buffalo to only ten shots on goal in the final 45 minutes. Ryan sat on his bench, half dressed, soaked with sweat. A small gash over his right eye was a souvenir of the rough evening.

Two reporters asked him about the game. "It was a battle of two hot goalies, one of our best games in the last few weeks," he replied between sips of apple juice. "We're not happy with a tie, but we're satisfied with our effort tonight."

It was midnight when Ryan and Jennifer left the Forum. After signing a few autographs, the centerman chuckled as he recalled the words of former teammate Steve Shutt, one of the Canadiens' all-time goal scorers who recently had been traded to Los Angeles. "Just before he left, he told me, 'The fans love you in this town, win or tie.' "

At the couple's three-hundred-year-old French cottage, Jennifer spread some Chinese food on a large dining table at one end of a great room that consisted of an open kitchen, a living area with a large stone fireplace and the dining area. Their seven-month-old boy, Benjamin, sat wide awake in his walker as they ate. "I'd been asking God for more time to pray," Jennifer said with a laugh. "So the baby started waking up in the middle of the night. It's really a great time to pray."

As they finished eating, Jennifer took Benjamin to another room while Ryan talked about the pressure of playing in Montreal. "Last year was the team's first losing season in more than thirty years. We all felt the pressure; it's not easy to go to the rink when you're losing. Everything seems harder. But it should be fun. After all, it's a game."

Hockey has been fun for most of Ryan's life. He was born in New Westminster and raised in Burnaby, British Columbia. He began playing hockey at age six, and at fifteen left home to play junior hockey — with the understanding that he kept up with school. "That was great for me because I didn't have much motivation. My grades went from average to honor roll because I had to think about what would happen if hockey didn't work out."

Ryan was his team's most valuable player and the league's player of the year, causing the Washington Capitals to make him their first choice and the league's second overall in the 1978 amateur draft. He scored 28 goals in his first NHL season, 24 in his second, and was voted team captain at age twenty-two, the youngest player so honored in the NHL. By the 81-82 season, Ryan had raised his scoring totals to 38 goals and 87 points. But something even more significant was happening in his life.

Before telling the story, Ryan went to the refrigerator to find some ice. He returned with a pack of frozen corn and placed it over a rapidly swelling right eye that had turned a purplish blue.

"When I was Washington's captain," he said, "Don Liesemer approached me about starting a chapel service for the team." Don, president of Hockey Ministries International, had won approval from league headquarters to start a chapel program. The idea was to hold 20- to 30-minute chapel services when players were unable to attend church because of Sunday games. Ryan was very open to Don's proposal — "If it would help my hockey!"

Ryan went to the first Sunday service out of curiosity

and ended up attending every meeting. "I always thought that if I was good, I would go to heaven . . . the better I was, the more God would accept me. But the speakers were saying that the Bible had a different message. We can never please God by our own efforts, and that is why He sent Jesus Christ to pay for our sins."

A few months after the chapels started, Jean Pronovost was traded to the Capitals. The coach was concerned about Jean's "religious views" and asked Ryan to keep an eye on the veteran right winger. Ryan watched and was intrigued by what he saw. Jean not only taught the young captain some new tricks on the ice, he invited Ryan and teammate Mike Gartner to study the Bible in his home. "Jean and his wife had a love, a security that had been brought about by the changes God had made in their lives. I thought Bible studies would be dull, but they were a lot of fun. And I was able to ask questions."

It took a year for Ryan to accept "God's free gift of salvation," as he describes it. "I think it was pride that held me back. I particularly wondered how it was going to affect my game. I didn't want it to make me less aggressive or . . . to take me out of the game and make me a missionary."

Pronovost encouraged Ryan to believe that God was big enough to trust with every detail of life. One afternoon before a game in Edmonton, under deep conviction, Ryan admitted his need for Jesus Christ, accepted His forgiveness for his sins, and invited Christ into his life.

Jennifer returned to the table, having nursed Benjamin to sleep. She told how Ryan's former coach with the Caps, Gary Green, introduced them while she was visiting her old Toronto employer for two days. That started a long-distance courtship that culminated the following fall when Ryan proposed. Jennifer laughed as she recalled that it was after a game in which he'd received another black eye.

They were married in June of 1982 and had just set up their home in Washington when they learned of the trade to Montreal right before the opening of training camp. Ryan told his wife the news, then left immediately for Montreal, leaving her to pack, sell the house and move.

For Ryan, the trade meant going from a franchise that had survived the summer only through a massive public relations effort to an institution that has won nearly one third of the National Hockey League's championships. Unfortunately, in Montreal, many fans felt their team had given up too much for Ryan and defenseman Rick Green.

At first, Ryan tried to prove his critics wrong. Only after a few hard weeks did it dawn on him that he was part of a team, and that no individual player wins the Stanley Cup. "I started to focus on helping the team win, and that relieved much of the pressure."

It wasn't so easy for Jennifer. "She's so loyal," said Ryan with a big smile as he removed the bag of corn from his eye. "One morning our clock radio came on and we heard the sports announcer cutting down the team. When he said I wasn't playing the way I should, Jen popped out of bed and said, 'That's not true!' "

The couple found their major source of support in a small church in the suburb of Pointe-Claire and in their friendship with Don and Jean Liesemer, and the Pronovosts who had joined the staff of Hockey Ministries International. They were able to get teaching from the Bible and develop friendships that carried them through the ups and downs of a season. "There are many wives on the team who don't socialize with anyone but other players' wives," Jennifer explained. "Hockey's such a transient thing. The church gives me friends I can count on no matter what happens in hockey." When Ryan was hurt in Pittsburgh, church friends immediately phoned Jennifer to offer support.

The Walters were convinced that God wanted them in Montreal, at least for the time being. They had chosen to live in the area all year, and Ryan had enrolled in French classes at a local language school. While they continued to develop their relationship with God, they also were looking for ways to share what they'd learned with others. Ryan spoke at a city-wide crusade, and at other smaller events, telling of his hope in Jesus Christ.

It was 3:30 in the morning when the conversation ended at the Walters' table. Ryan's boyish smile said that he had enjoyed the discussion. As he took Aslan, his large golden retriever, out for a quick romp in the snow, he mentioned that his relationship with God was now a natural part of his life. "More than anything, I want to tell people, 'Look what I've found!' Maybe they will laugh at me, but I find the Christian life exciting!"

Mike Gartner

2
MIKE GARTNER

Twenty minutes into practice, the sun finally broke through the clouds and poured into the Mt. Vernon Sports Complex. The Washington Capitals, despite a game the previous night, were going through a strenuous morning workout. For the next two hours, coach Bryan Murray pushed his team up and down the ice with numerous drills. Right winger Mike Gartner, the previous night's number one star, worked hard, pausing only occasionally to lean against the boards and grab a squirt of water.

There were high hopes for this team at the start of the season; many believed they were capable of challenging for the Stanley Cup. But over their first fourteen games, they'd won only five and stood uncomfortably in fourth place in the tough Patrick Division. Last night, the Caps had held one-goal leads three times, only to wind up with a tie. It was a game they should have won.

After practice, several players remained on the ice for additional work while the coach met with reporters. The first question concerned the intensity of the practice. "We're working hard," said Murray, "but we have mental lapses. So I thought we'd tighten up and go hard for a while and see if it pays off."

As Mike skated off the ice, he heard the comment and whispered, "I think he's mad at us." Sweat was streaming down his face and his practice jersey was soaked. But his expression seemed to say that he didn't mind the hard work — it would soon pay dividends. Mike said he'd be ready for lunch after a quick shower.

As Gartner headed into the locker room, Coach Murray talked about his star right winger, who along with Bob Carpenter was leading the team in scoring. "When I first came here, Mike was a great skater and a great breakaway type player. But he was a little erratic in puck handling and shooting. Mentally, he didn't have the maturity to take advantage of the great skill he had."

Mike's skill was evident by 1984 in his career records, as he led the Capitals in games played and goals scored, and was second in assists and total points.

His goal production, however, had dipped slightly

for several years after Murray took over the Caps' reins in November of 1981.

Soon after he became coach, Murray made his troops develop a more defensive style of play. "If you don't get them young, it's tough to make them adjust," he said. "Sometimes a guy ends up shortening his career because when he loses speed, he can't check or do some of the other things you have to do to win. So Mike did sacrifice a bit on offense, but he upgraded his defense. He showed what a real player he is by sacrificing himself for the good of the team. Now, we need some of that offense back, so we're starting to free him up a bit more." Not only did Murray's coaching benefit Mike's defense, but it enabled the Capitals to leave behind their lowly past and become a playoff team.

Mike's game got another boost in a recent off-season as he played for Team Canada in a Canada Cup victory over the Soviet Union and Sweden. In the process, he studied the world's top players and implemented some new moves and puck control skills. "I've worked extra hard moving the puck along the boards in our end," he said in a *Washington Post* story. He also improved his shooting. "I'm taking better shots, not so many low percentage shots."

Mike emerged from the locker room and said he would be delayed for a few minutes by a team meeting. As player representative for the Caps, he'd invited a financial consultant to give some advice to the players. Once that business was completed, we headed out to a nearby restaurant.

While waiting for hamburgers, Mike talked about his hobby — reading. "I enjoy James Michener and Leon Uris. I read Christian books by men like Billy Graham and Hal Lindsey and a wide variety of novels. Last year, I read *The Grapes of Wrath* by John Steinbeck. I think that book made a real impact. It opened my eyes to see how badly people can treat each other."

As he sipped a cola, Mike reflected on the fact that he didn't study hard in school — "I just went through the motions." He was trying to make up for it now, though, taking courses at the University of Maryland. In the second year of a six-year Capitals' contract, he hoped to use his free time to get a degree and prepare for a second career.

"It was really foolish not to study hard in school," he said matter-of-factly as our food arrived. "When you're fourteen or fifteen, you don't know what's going to happen. School is an excellent backup, a safety factor. If something happens in hockey, you have something to fall back on."

Mike's reading hobby carries his learning beyond the classroom. "I never used to read," he admitted. "When I had to read in school, I read the condensed notes. But after I started playing professional hockey, I saw how much time I had, especially on road trips. I could sit around and watch TV, or I could use the time to learn. I started reading, and enjoyed it. In fact, I really limit my TV watching now."

Gartner was born in Ottawa, the youngest of five

children. The family moved a number of times within Ontario, but that didn't affect Mike's hockey. He started skating at age three and played on his first team at five. As a teenager, he led the Barrie Flyers to the Wrigley Midget Hockey Championship and represented Canada at a tournament in Russia.

Blessed with natural speed — he's one of the fastest skaters in the NHL — Mike further developed his skills at power skating schools. He played two years of Junior A hockey, then signed a contract with Cincinnati of the World Hockey Association. That was primarily an economic decision: "I made $75 a week playing for the Niagara Falls Flyers. Cincinnati offered me $75,000 a year."

Mike was drafted in the first round by the Caps in 1979 and was the fourth player chosen overall. Initially that was a disappointment; he wanted to play in Detroit, just a short drive from the University of Western Ontario where his wife-to-be was studying. Eventually, he warmed to the idea that Washington was a young, up-and-coming team. As a rookie, only twenty years old, he won the team's Most Valuable Player award.

Despite all his success, with its corresponding benefits — a large salary, a home, a fancy car — Mike began to sense that he really wasn't fulfilled in life. "I was a happy person, yet there was a void. I realized it when Jean Pronovost joined our team."

Jean was a veteran of thirteen NHL seasons and ranked among the NHL's top twenty-five career goal scorers. His strength of character made the same kind of impact on Gartner that it had on Ryan Walter. "He showed me a lot of friendship," said Mike. "He was a right wing too, and he taught me some tricks. I noticed he was always level; he didn't have the ups and downs the rest of us had. And he was always smiling. His wife was the same way."

Jean and Diane Pronovost invited Mike and his teammates to participate in a Bible study at their home. Mike had attended church as a boy because his parents required it. But thinking that church was a meaningless exercise, he dropped it as a teenager. What he heard in this Bible study was new to him.

"I knew there was life after death," he explained. "But I never really thought about the fact that there is a heaven and a hell, and we have to make a decision that will determine where we spend eternity. One day on an airplane, Jean asked me, 'Mike, if this plane went down and you died right now, would you go to heaven or hell?' I had to say that I didn't know for sure. He showed me from the Bible that I was a sinner, separated from God. The only way to know God was through Jesus Christ. He came to earth, died for my sins, and rose again from the dead. I could either accept Him or reject Him, but if I didn't accept Him, that meant I was rejecting Him.

"I certainly didn't want to go to hell. And I knew there was something missing in my life. In a hotel room in the middle of that road trip, I got on my knees and said, 'Lord, if You're real, come into my life right now and

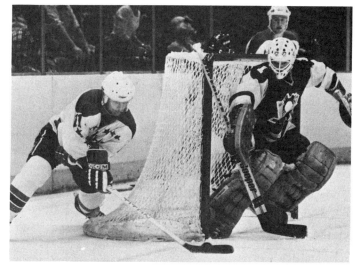

Mike Gartner established himself as a bona fide all-star with more than 50 goals in the 1984-85 season.

change me.' Almost immediately, I had a feeling of relief, and of expectation."

Mike's life began to change in the following months. "I used to swear a lot, and that was taken away. It wasn't something I changed on my own; I knew I couldn't do that. The Lord just took it away. I used to drink a lot and I had some close calls — once I drove home from a party and the next day I couldn't remember that 15-minute drive. God took away my desire for alcohol. I still like to go out with the guys, but I just drink Coke."

The changes caused conflict with Mike's fiancée, Colleen. She had liked Mike the way he was, and the changes shook her up. They had some of their worst arguments in the weeks immediately following Mike's conversion. She was ready to call off their wedding, but Mike prayed that God would change her. One night she told him, "Well, I've done it, too." She had made her decision for Christ. They were married that summer in a beautiful Christian ceremony.

The greatest area of change in Mike, and the one that convinced Colleen of the reality of Christ, was in his temper. Almost immediately, he became more patient, more sensitive to others around him. "Before, I didn't think about my temper, or swearing, or drinking. It was all second nature. But after I became a Christian, something inside me said, 'Hey, these things aren't right.' "

Mike feels his conversion had a positive effect on his hockey, particularly in his motivation for the sport. "I'm playing to glorify God, and I think the way I can do that is to play my best. I just signed a long-term contract [six years] before this season. Maybe before I would have sat back and said, 'I've got it made for six years, so I can cruise,' but now, I feel very responsible to God."

Perhaps the greatest test of Mike's faith came in 1983 when a puck struck him flush in his left eye during a game against Winnipeg. At first, there was no fear of permanent damage. Then tests revealed a fractured cheek and damage to his optic nerve. The eye was receiving images but wasn't sending proper messages to the brain. Mike couldn't drive a car, much less play hockey.

He admits that those days were difficult for him and Colleen. "We both had to trust the Lord, that He knew what He was doing. Before, I'm sure I would have panicked. But I said, 'Lord, this is in Your control. There's nothing we can do, nothing the doctors can do.'"

Three weeks later, Mike was playing again — with a protective shield attached to his helmet to protect his eyes. He continues to wear the shield and will for the remainder of his career.

"That has been our biggest test," he said of the incident. "I praise God that He worked things out the way I wanted. Maybe next time it won't be that way. Still, Colleen and I only want what He wants. We realize that whatever happens, He is in control; it's not left to chance."

As we left the restaurant, Mike said that he takes half an hour every morning to be alone with God. ("And it should be an hour!") He spends the time reading the Bible and praying. In addition, he prays each night with his wife before going to sleep.

"God's been teaching me to depend on Him," he said about his daily quiet time. "He wants me to be more faithful, to keep Him first in everything. I'm having a good year and I'm trying to keep from patting myself on the back. The reason I'm playing is to glorify God. I've been thinking about that a lot lately. I want people to see that God has given me the skills and the confidence to play well."

Mike's skill was evident to all who followed the team. And the hard work was paying off, too, as the team began to roll up wins. In one twenty-game stretch, the Capitals won sixteen and tied two, moving them into first place in their division. Mike's scoring pace would lead to a 50-goal season and it put him in the all-star game. But the personal accomplishments weren't enough. Mike was now a complete player, able to hold his own on both offense and defense. He wanted to see those skills used to help the Caps advance through the playoffs to a Stanley Cup title.

Paul Baxter

3
PAUL BAXTER

Several large blocks of ice loomed to our left as the taxi sped past the Place du Palais. In a few weeks, that ice would be transformed into a majestic snow castle, part of Quebec's famous Winter Carnival. We passed through one of the gates of the old city wall and down the narrow Rue Saint-Louis to the Restaurant Continental. We paused briefly to gaze up at the Chateau Frontenac, it's many green-roofed turrets brightly lit in the cold winter sky, before dashing into the cozy French restaurant.

For Paul Baxter, a trip to Quebec brought back many memories. He'd played four seasons in this city, three of them in the old World Hockey Association, the fourth after the merger with the NHL. His oldest daughter, Nicole, was born here. Now as a defenseman for the Calgary Flames, Paul was making his only regular season visit to the city.

Don Liesemer, whose friendship with Paul extended back to those days in Quebec, inquired about the open sore on the knuckle of Paul's left forefinger. "I hit someone," he admitted sheepishly; then hastily added, "but it was only my second fight all year."

In earlier seasons, two fights in a single game were not uncommon for Paul. He was well-known for his aggressive play and large amount of penalty minutes. His 1981-82 time in the penalty box was the second highest in league history. But that total had dropped remarkably in the past three years, and he no longer even led his team in penalties. Current league statistics showed him no higher than thirty-sixth in that category. Obviously, some things had changed in Paul Baxter's style of play.

Selecting our meal was a half-hour process, involving several consultations with the waiter. Paul finally settled on pheasant with an appetizer of escargot. "I really enjoyed living here," Paul said as we waited for our meals. "Hockey is the only major sport in this town. Julie and I had just married when I came here. It was a hard adjustment, especially the communication barrier. There was only one English-speaking TV station."

Paul, while not totally fluent in French, is now comfortable in the language and shifted easily between

English and French as he talked with Don and the waiter. "Did you know I'm writing a column?" he asked as the main course arrived. "I'm doing one a week for the *Calgary Sun* and I enjoy it."

"Is someone helping you write it?" Don asked.

"Nope. I write it myself. I print it on Sunday night, turn it in Monday and they do the rest. They've done very little editing."

"What have you written about?"

"Violence. The adjustments when your career is over. I gave my picks for the all-star game. I must be doing something right. Fischler blasted me in *The Hockey News*." Stan Fischler, the New York-based hockey writer, had headlined his latest column "If You Report, Baxter, Give Me The Facts." Stan had objected to Paul's reference to violence by certain unnamed members of the Edmonton Oilers. He suggested Paul take a basic university reporting class and learn how to name names.

Paul laughed off the criticism. "I wasn't trying to attack the Oilers or any other individuals," he explained. "I was making some general observations about the game."

Conversation drifted to the events that brought Don and Paul together during the 1978 Christmas season. Paul told how Nordique goalie Michel Dion had stood in the middle of the dressing room and announced that there would be a chapel service the next Sunday. He asked how many players were interested. "My hand shot up immediately," said Paul. "There was definitely curiosity and wonderment from my teammates who had always regarded me as a bit of a hell-raiser. Not only were they surprised, I was surprised that I raised my hand."

Approximately half the team turned out for that service, and Don was the speaker. Paul speculates that the Christmas season had something to do with the turnout. The second service, shortly after New Year's Day, was attended only by Michel, Paul and the coach.

"I'll never forget your first message," Paul said to Don. "It was the story of Jesus and the disciples in the boat. Jesus fell asleep and there was a big storm and the waves were pounding agaisnt the boat and the apostles became worried and started yelling for Jesus to help them."

"That was the second message, Paul."

"Then I remember the second message. The first I don't remember."

"After my talk, you started asking lots of questions. You wanted to know if you had to stop drinking and swearing if you became a Christian."

"I was going through a difficult period. That second meeting, I felt so peaceful when we were talking. Then you explained how I could know Christ. I readily accepted. I asked Christ into my life and felt really comfortable with the decision."

Paul's problems at that time included an erratic

career and a knee injury that team officials assumed would limit his long-term effectiveness as a player. Ironically, according to Paul, "My career didn't take off until I received Christ."

A dessert tray was brought to the table, and Paul selected the strawberry shortcake. "It was my priorities that changed," he explained. "When hockey was my number one priority, I was concerned about what everyone thought about me. I was kind of insecure. I'd do almost anything to impress people. I was boisterous. Afterward, I wasn't playing for myself anymore. I was playing for a greater Master, so I was less interested in what others thought of me."

"What about Julie's reaction?" Don asked.

"E.T.," Paul said, shaking his head. "It was perfectly understandable. You've been married to one person for a long time and all of a sudden his ideals and priorities change."

"She noticed the changes?"

"I got really quiet for about a month. Meditative. I was not the gregarious individual I was before. Don, remember how I called you a couple of times? I told you about some of the things I'd done in the past, and I wasn't sure that God would forgive them. You reassured me.

"Julie is an unbelievably dedicated person. When I became a Christian, she didn't want to be pushed into it. But every night she read the Bible, and I don't think she had done that before. It was about a month later that she received Christ, too."

After dessert, we headed back to the hotel where the Flames were staying. In Don's room, we looked north over the glittering lights of the city and talked about Paul's reputation as a player, in particular one season in Pittsburgh. Although Paul had trusted in Christ by that time, he still amassed 409 penalty minutes. "I stuck my nose in a lot of areas where it didn't belong," he said, stretching out on one of the two queen-size beds. "I also said a lot of things when there wasn't any need for talk. Consequently, I antagonized a lot of players and referees, and that cost me a lot of penalty minutes."

Paul was obviously uncomfortable with this topic, yet he patiently answered the questions. "Did you feel your job was to protect your teammates? Or were you simply playing too aggressively?"

"There are two issues here. One is sticking up for teammates. That can generate penalty minutes. On the other hand, there are a lot of cases where if I would have kept my mouth shut . . . I think I hurt my Christian testimony. I lacked some self-control and discretion. I don't feel there's anything wrong with being an aggressive play and dirty play. There are times I've that year, I kind of lost touch with my purpose as a hockey player. It was to play aggressively, but not to be antagonistic."

"At what point do the penalties begin hurting the team?"

Once accumulating penalty minutes at a near-record level, Paul Baxter now has "cleaned up his act" remarkably.

"A lot of people would say that there aren't any penalties that are beneficial to a team. I guess I would agree to a certain extent. But there are also times when, if your team is being intimidated, or you feel a smaller team member is being taken advantage of, I'm not so sure that's the time to hide. It's a team sport. I still wrestle with those arguments within myself. God has obviously done a great work in that area, helping me to distinguish what the right and wrong times are."

"Have you ever considered yourself a dirty player?"

"At times. Without a doubt there is a fine line between aggressive play and dirty play. There are times I've overstepped those boundaries. In the last two or three years, I think I've learned where that fine line is."

"You say God has changed you in this area. How has He done that?"

"I don't know. I think He understands our weaknesses. I think He wants to deal with those areas in our lives if we are willing to ask Him to help us. Obviously that was a problem for me. It was quite embarrassing, actually, to profess to be a Christian and lead the NHL in penalty minutes. A lot of Christians saw that as a contradiction."

"In fact, a number of people have questioned how you can be a Christian."

"That bothers me to be judged by other Christians. I'm not perfect. But anyone who's around me for any period of time hopefully knows that I love Jesus Christ. Some of the things I do wrong are more obvious than some of the things they do. I don't get a chance to look in their house every night and see how they're living."

"Have you ever felt the need to apologize to an opponent?"

"Yeah, if I feel I've wronged an opponent needlessly. Which I guess would be most times. I'm not shy about saying I'm sorry."

"Have you ever intentionally tried to hurt someone?"

"Never. That's a big word. I should say I can't recall going into a game saying I'm going to get a certain guy. I don't carry grudges."

"Do you feel the press has branded you unfairly?"

"To be quite frank, what the press writes bothers me a lot of times. Sometimes they write about hearsay. I've never been suspended, but one year there were three incidents where another guy was suspended and I was the victim in all three cases. Perhaps because they happened in big media capitals, I was branded as the perpetrator. In two of the cases, I hit the guys hard but clean, and they went after me, and all of a sudden it's my fault because they got suspended."

"What about fighting? Do you feel there are times when you have to fight?"

"I try not to fight unless I'm threatened or a teammate is threatened. For instance, the other night in Chicago, I was defending a three-on-two rush. Our other defenseman got the puck and one of their players cross-checked me into the goal post. For no reason. I hadn't touched the puck. I was upset and I lost my temper."

"You still play aggressively?"

"That's right. It benefits the team when I play aggressively. But again, there's a fine line. I try not to step over it."

It was nearly midnight, curfew time for the Calgary players. Paul was thoughtful now, not joking as he had earlier in the evening. He told about an incident the previous summer that has profoundly affected his life. "There haven't been many things go wrong with my life. I mean, I haven't had a family member die, or anyone seriously sick. Until Laura, my youngest. She was seventeen months old and she wasn't growing. It was diagnosed in Pittsburgh as a heart defect. When we came to Calgary, Cliff Fletcher [the Flames' general manager] lined up the doctors to take care of her. She had one operation in Calgary in June, and a second one in Vancouver in August.

"I would have felt a lot calmer if she hadn't had to have surgery. But God gave us peace of mind, an inner confidence that He was going to do what was best. And to see how she's responded, it's incredible. I'm so thankful I could watch how God has worked in her life. She's doing fantastic now. She beats up her brother."

Paul admitted that it was not easy for him to maintain his Christian commitment. "I really drifted in November and December, as far as my closeness to God. But you know it's as if He has you on a rope, and He'll only let you out so far and then, as any good father, He's a great disciplinarian . . . I've come to terms with that and gotten back to being close to Him."

Sitting up on the edge of the bed, Paul thought for a moment as we prepared to leave. "There is such a tremendous source of joy when we stay close to him." He shook his head. "We may give up on God at times, but thankfully He never gives up on us."

Dan Bouchard

---- 4 ----

DAN BOUCHARD

T he Colisée, home of the Quebec Nordiques, was
virtually empty, save for a few reporters waiting
for the visiting team to take a light morning skate
prior to the game that night. The home team had just
finished its workout, and the only player still on the ice
was a goalie, in full pads, doing sprints across the width
of the rink.

The player was Dan Bouchard, a veteran of thirteen
NHL seasons. Two nights earlier, he'd tended goal in a
losing effort against Edmonton. Tonight, he would back
up Richard Sevigny, who was getting a rare start. As
usual on such days, Bouchard did extra work to maintain
peak conditioning. He'd been on the ice before most of

his teammates, stopping orange street-hockey balls to keep his reflexes sharp.

Later, when the Calgary Flames were in the middle of their workout, Dan emerged from the Quebec dressing room, wearing jeans and a white sweater with red and blue stripes on the sleeves. Ignoring the action on the ice, he told his guests about his season thus far. "I've had some bad luck at home," he said. "I'm five and eight, but in the eight losses, the team has scored only 12 goals." He didn't have to say that it's tough to win when you must hold the opposition to less than 2 goals every game. On the road, his record was better — only one loss against five wins and three ties. His goals against average was a very respectable 3.11.

That morning, the paper *Quebec Le SoLeil* had run a story about Dan and his diligent efforts to be the best goaltender possible. Recalling what he'd said in the interview, Dan told us, "At thirty-four, I have to work harder to be in good condition." Dan explained that he also was developing improved equipment, including shoulder pads and gloves for goalies. With pride, he noted that several NHL goalies were now using equipment he had designed.

Dan suggested lunch at a favorite Italian restaurant, so we left the arena. Once in his four-wheel-drive vehicle, he decided to conduct a quick, impromptu tour of old Quebec. We drove through the narrow streets to the Lower Town on the banks of the St. Lawrence River, momentarily forgetting about a friend who was trying vainly to follow.

With one hand lightly on the wheel, Dan pointed out the difference between the French and English architecture in this 450-year-old city. We passed the Place Royale where Champlain founded the first permanent French settlement in 1608, and Dan pointed up to the Séminaire de Québec, perched on the ridge overlooking the river. "It's the oldest seminary in North America," he explained. With our friend again following us, we wound back up Côte-de-la-Montagne for a closer look at the seminary and the Basilica of Notre-Dame, built by the Jesuits in 1647.

A few blocks later, still within the old walls, we found our restaurant, La Crémaillère. "I recommend the frog legs," he said as we were seated. Dan is knowledgeable about food and enjoys cooking. "French and Italian food," he said. "I love to fix Fettucini Alfredo. And I cook escargot, chopped and sauteed in butter and covered with a white sauce."

Dan switched effortlessly between French and English as he talked with the waiters and visited with his friends. His enthusiasm for life is magnified by piercing eyes and sharp Nordic features. Dan's personality is infectious, whether he's talking about Quebec's history, his favorite foods, or hockey in this one-sport city.

"People get very angry when we lose to the Canadiens," he said. "To show you how hockey-oriented this community is, when we play the Canadiens in the playoffs, the water level drops dramatically between periods. No one leaves the television to go to the washroom until the period is over.

"We have just a tiny airport, and five thousand people were waiting for us when we beat Montreal in the playoffs in 1982. Hockey means everything here."

The rivalry between Quebec and Montreal is one of the most intense in all of sport and has been fueled by the fact that the two teams meet eight times each regular season. The intensity began during the Nordiques' third season in the NHL when they met the Canadiens in the Adams Division semifinal. Quebec won three games to two on an overtime goal by Dale Hunter in the Montreal Forum.

During another divisional playoff between the two teams, Quebec lost in six fierce games. Newspapers in the two cities fueled the emotions of fans by devoting as many as ten pages to the series each day. It was no longer just a sports event; it became a major news story, and the players reflected that with a physical level of play rarely seen even in hockey. Much as he hates to lose, Bouchard admits he was glad the series did not go to a seventh game. "It would have been a blood bath," he said, shaking his head.

One does not conduct an interview with Dan Bouchard. You can ask him questions, but he'll take you wherever he wants to go, warmly revealing insights into his style as a player, his religious heritage and the effect his faith has on his life today.

Dan was born in Vald'or, Quebec, and was raised in Montreal where his father worked for twenty-five years in a brewery after playing professional hockey under Eddie Shore. "My father died four years ago, after playing a fun game," said Dan. "He knew hockey inside out, and he died the way he wanted." He speaks reverently of his father, even as he reveals that the man had a fierce temper. "He loved to argue. Very obstinate. You'd tell him that wall was black and if he saw one speck of white on it, he'd say it was a white wall."

Dan inherited that argumentative nature, and in his eight seasons with the Atlanta Flames he was branded a troublemaker. "I was very cocky. There was always a good reason why I let in a goal. It was never my fault. I would tell the guys, 'Listen, if you'd move your butt, we'd be winning.' They don't want to hear that."

But the team put up with Dan's attitude because he was an effective goalie. He perfected a butterfly style of play, taking away the ice and forcing opponents to shoot high where he usually was able to snag the puck with his quick hands. He was also not afraid to wander into the corners for a loose puck.

When the Flames moved to Calgary prior to the 80-81 season, Dan felt ready for an even greater change — he desperately wanted to leave the Flames. He was frustrated by communication problems on the team, and his teammates were equally frustrated with his temperamental nature. He played infrequently, and for the first time, his goals-against average drifted above 4. As the team left on a two-week road trip, Dan was left behind and informed that a trade was imminent.

The news thrilled him, until the general manager

Goalie Dan Bouchard, a veteran of thirteen NHL seasons, is seeing other goaltenders adopt new equipment he has designed.

phoned to say that the deal had fallen through. That sent Dan into depression. "I felt I was on the verge of a nervous breakdown," he said. "I had everything material, but I wasn't happy. My dad had taught me what reality was, but all of a sudden, reality was that I wasn't happy. My pride was crushed."

Dan's wife, Jan, assuming her husband would be on the road trip, had gone to visit relatives in Ontario. Dan called her and cried as he talked with her by phone. She suggested he pray.

Jan's advice was not difficult for Dan to accept, for he had grown up in a very religious home. He attended church every Sunday, even after he became a professional hockey player. "If I didn't go to church on Sunday, something was missing. I always prayed, but I would try to use God to get things, like we use cash to buy a chocolate bar. It was mostly a ritual."

That night, with his wife in Ontario and his teammates on the road, Dan faced himself for the first time. He opened the Bible and began to read. It was like a mirror revealing to him his cockiness. "It was like I was walking with the sun always behind me, and I kept running into a wall caused by the shadow of my pride. I couldn't climb out of it, until I turned around and faced the sun."

The sun was the Son of God, Jesus Christ, who had paid the price for sin through His death and resurrection. That night, Dan was deeply upset as he realized how he had displeased God. But he accepted Christ's forgiveness and surrendered control of his life to the Savior. Things began to change immediately. "The next morning I got up and said, 'Lord, what do we do now?' I went down to the rink and the coach of the junior team walked by. I suddenly asked him if I could practice with his team. If I'd slapped him in the face, he couldn't have been more shocked."

For two weeks Dan practiced with the junior team. That experience was symbolic of the death of his pride, and it even helped his play, as he found himself getting some much-needed practice.

When Dan's teammates returned, they were surprised at the change. "I told them, 'I accepted the Lord and I'm going to go His way.' " But change or not, Dan's days with the Flames were numbered. He was called into the office of the general manager, Cliff Fletcher, and told a trade was pending with Quebec. "The Nordiques were in last place, but only eight points out of a playoff spot. I told the Quebec GM, Maurice Filion, I thought we could make the playoffs. I was in good shape and would bring him a good body. I promised him there would be no problems. I just wanted to play hockey like I thought I could."

And play he did. After the trade, Dan appeared in twenty-nine games, and the Nordiques won nineteen, along with five ties. He recorded two shutouts and a goals-against average of 3.17, propelling the team to a fourth-place finish. He recorded another shutout in the first round playoff series against Philadelphia, but it was not enough to prevent Quebec's elimination at the hands of the Flyers.

By the time we talked at La Crémaillère, Dan was at home in Quebec, playing his fifth season with the team and in the third year of a five-year contract. Despite his age, he felt sharper than ever, and wanted to become even better. "The Lord says 'buffet your body,' " Dan said, quoting from the New Testament book of 1 Corinthians. "I'm to make my body my slave. I'm to run in order to win, exercising self-control."

Among the things he's done is to study the training techniques of the Russians and their outstanding goaltender, Vladislav Tretiak, now retired. "He quit because it was push, push, push," said Dan, implying that he has learned to temper his physical training in order to avoid burnout.

The spiritual dimension has also aided his play. He explained that at least 75 percent of his job is concentration and anticipation, and that his faith has helped relieve the mental pressure. "I don't think you should feel the pressure; after all, Christ lives in you. That makes a world of difference." He cited how in the previous three games, opponents had scored on their first shot. "They were good shots. But I've got 59 more minutes to play, so I'm not going to quit."

Contrary to the past, he was even willing to admit his mistakes as a net minder. "My job is to anticipate, and some nights you anticipate a fraction of a second too fast and beat yourself. A goalie beats himself more than a player beats him. Some nights my timing is perfect. Other nights, I over-anticipate. It's like a baseball player anticipating a fastball and he gets beat on a slow curve."

As far as a teammate not doing his job — "That's not for me to judge. The coaches have videos and they can decide who goofed."

You can't spend much time with Dan Bouchard without sensing his feeling of mission in life. He tells a story about his mother and how she prayed for him as a boy. "I was five days old, and I was dying. The doctors put me in an incubator and gave me a blood transfusion. My mom tells me that she went to church and told the Lord I was His if He would save me."

It took many years for Dan to establish a true relationship with God, but now he wants to be a witness for the faith. He talked fondly of becoming a full-time Christian worker after his career ends. But he was not waiting for retirement in order to start sharing the gospel — he was already busy telling about his faith throughout Quebec City. He had a two-minute radio show every Saturday in which he read brief selections from various Christian classics. And he spoke at schools and visited hospitals.

He particularly enjoyed talking with young people, and he encouraged them to delve into the Bible. "I was speaking a few days ago," he said, "and a boy asked me, 'Why do you read the Bible?' I told him it was a very good way to talk with the Lord. Do you realize that there are 3,400 promises in this book? People are looking for something in life, just like I was. They will find what they are looking for in the Bible because that's how God communicates with us."

Doug Jarvis

5

DOUG JARVIS

The cold November wind was the chief signal of impending winter. Many of the trees were bare, but the remaining leaves painted a few splashes of red and orange on a gray, cloudy day. It felt good to step inside the warm, colonial-style town house, home of Doug Jarvis, a centerman for the Washington Capitals. In a few hours, Doug would play his 734th consecutive regular season NHL game, the third longest streak in hockey history.

In the kitchen, Doug's wife, Linda, was preparing the pre-game dinner. Their three-month-old baby, Laura, was asleep in the living room, so Doug and his guest quietly slipped downstairs. There, on the mantle of the fireplace in his family room, sat a silver bowl, the

Selke Trophy, awarded each year to the league's outstanding defensive forward. Doug had won it for the 1983-84 season, thus finally gaining public recognition for the skills that had helped his teams take seven consecutive division titles and four Stanley Cup championships. But beyond the Selke Trophy, the Jarvis home contains few tangible reminders of Doug's outstanding NHL career.

The lack of flashy trophies symbolizes Doug's personality. For years, he has toiled quietly, winning crucial faceoffs, checking the opponent's top line and killing penalties, while other teammates scored the goals and received the glory. He played seven seasons with the Montreal Canadiens, and four of those years they were Stanley Cup champions. Now with the Capitals, he, along with former Canadiens Rod Langway and Craig Laughlin, has helped turn a perennial doormat into one of the league's toughest teams. The Selke award showed that Doug's peers now recognized his considerable talents.

But when you talk about Doug Jarvis, you don't just talk about talent. You also talk about endurance. Sport's most famous iron man was Lou Gehrig, a powerful 212-pound first baseman who played 2,130 consecutive games for the New York Yankees. Doug, however, doesn't fit that image of raw power. He stands only 5'9" and weighs 165. Surely in nine-plus years of battling for pucks in the corners and absorbing vicious body checks, he should have suffered at least one injury to keep him out of action.

"I've been very fortunate," he said quietly. "It's one of those things I don't think about a whole lot. I just think about one game at a time. I can't think of one time where there was doubt about whether I should play or not."

An analysis of Jarvis' game reveals other key qualities. He has a keen mind for the game of hockey and helps Bryan Murray as an unofficial assistant coach, viewing video tapes of opponents in order to discover ways to defeat them. And then there's his unselfishness. "With the character he has," Murray once told the *Washington Post*, "Doug Jarvis exemplifies the type of person who puts the team ahead of the individual. He will sacrifice the body and take a check every time to be sure the puck gets out of the (defensive) zone."

At first it appeared that Doug would spend his career in Ontario, near his hometown of Brantford. He played two years of Junior A hockey for Peterborough. After scoring 133 points in sixty-four games in his second season, he was drafted by the Toronto Maple Leafs. It looked like the perfect situation. Toronto was close to home and needed centermen. It was a chance to jump immediately into the big leagues.

But before he ever donned a Maple Leaf jersey, Doug was traded to the Canadiens. "It was a big surprise," he says, "and I had mixed reactions. Most of their players spend two or three years in the minors. I knew it was an excellent organization, but I was concerned about whether or not I'd have an opportunity to play." In recent years, only two players had moved

At the end of the 1984-85 season Doug Jarvis became the "iron man" of hockey, with more than 800 consecutive games played.

directly from junior hockey to the Canadiens. Both were legends — Guy Lafleur and Henri Richard.

In the fall of 1975, Doug was the only rookie to make the Canadiens' squad. And he'd made it primarily because he'd mastered the game's fundamentals in junior hockey. Despite his impressive point totals in Junior A, he was more than a scorer. He was a complete player. The Canadiens paired him with two other defensive forwards to check their opponents' top scoring lines. The Canadiens won the Stanley Cup that season and the following three years. In 1982, Doug won the Fourth Star Trophy as the Canadiens' unsung hero.

Doug's trade to Washington came after three disappointing seasons for the Canadiens, years in which they won division titles but stumbled in the playoffs. In Montreal, anything less than a Stanley Cup was a poor season. A shakeup seemed necessary. The Canadiens sent Jarvis, all-star defenseman Rod Langway, Craig Laughlin and Brian Engblom to the Caps in exchange for Washington's captain, Ryan Walter, and defenseman Rick Green.

Jarvis wasn't completely surprised. "You never expect to spend your career in one city, and I saw there were a number of younger players coming up, especially centermen. But it's never easy leaving, especially after playing seven years in one city. You've built a lot of friendships and you're moving to something completely new."

The contrast was stark. Montreal had won twenty

Cups; Washington had never even qualified for the playoffs. Hockey was king in Montreal; in Washington, it served mainly as a consolation for sports fans who couldn't get tickets to see football's Redskins. In Montreal, the Canadiens always expected to win; in Washington, the Capitals wondered if they were good enough to even compete.

"When you haven't experienced winning, you don't know how it feels," Doug explained. "This team needed to win a few games and gain confidence." In his first Capitals' season, Doug's teammates got their first taste of playoff action. The next year, they lost to the New York Islanders through five tough games in the division finals. Now, some experts were predicting they would make the Cup finals. An emphasis on defense and fundamentals had transformed the team from its earlier dark days.

Linda called us to lunch. It was Doug's typical game-day meal: a small steak, salad and a generous serving of spaghetti. Doug drank vegetable juice while Linda sipped a cola. As we finished eating, Linda told how they had met at a church camp while he was in junior hockey. "I liked him right away, but Doug didn't show any interest," she said. "At first I thought he was conceited; later I realized he was shy. But I sensed there was something special under the surface."

Doug and Linda grew up on opposite ends of Ontario. They readily admit that their faith was the primary factor that drew them together, though nearly four years passed before they started dating. "My Mom and Dad wanted me in church each Sunday," said Doug. "At the age of twelve, at a church camp, I made a commitment to Christ. I knew I was a Christian at that point, but I didn't realize the importance of that decision until my late teens, when I wanted to make my whole life available to Him. I wanted Christ to have the freedom to guide me in any direction, whether it was hockey, or whatever."

Linda's story parallels her husband's. "I was taught to seek God's will in everything. I received Christ when I was seven or eight years old, but the real turning point came when I was eighteen. That's when I realized that being a Christian was a total commitment. Sometimes I think my testimony is boring, but I wouldn't trade it for anything."

Their faith affected their relationship from the beginning. Doug was in no rush to marry, wanting to be sure he had found the right girl. He admits that when he dated, "I just went out to have fun as a friend. I felt God would bring the right person along and until then, I looked at dating for friendship, without any pressure."

Linda chuckles at the explanation. "Doug's methodical. He thinks things through. I felt almost immediately that he was God's choice for me. But I prayed about it, because I wanted it to be God's relationship."

For Linda, the fact that Doug was committed to Jesus Christ was a critical factor, but at first she didn't realize how significant it was. "I looked at it as just another 'like.' When you first date, you compare your likes: you both like sports, or chocolate cake, or certain kinds of music. Now I realize that everything stems from our faith. God is the one who has glued us together."

"The longer we went out, the deeper the feelings became," added Doug. "I think there's an advantage when you take your time and build a friendship. The relationship is more solid when you get married. We didn't start dating until I was twenty-five, and it was another two years before we got married."

That was in July of 1982, and two months later Doug was traded. It was Linda's welcome to the world of professional sport, and she's thankful that her relationships with God and Doug were strong. "I knew no one in Washington. But Doug and I knew each other so well that it helped make the transition easier. We had to count on each other. Things don't always go as you want, or as you plan. But I've learned to have a childlike faith that God is in control, so I don't worry. God says He will take care of us. That doesn't mean it will always be roses. But He does have a plan."

Doug accepts full responsibility to serve as the spiritual leader in his home. "My wife looks to me to be the spiritual head . . . I'm very concerned that I am the person God wants me to be. Sometimes it's hard to maintain that priority, especially during the season when you can't always go to church on Sunday mornings. If I'm going to be the spiritual leader, I have to spend time daily reading the Bible, because it's our relationship with Christ that makes our lives complete."

Sometimes Doug feels like a rookie in the Christian life, but the example of his parents has helped. He applies the kind of discipline that makes him successful in hockey to his spiritual life. That means spending time every day studying the Bible and learning how his faith applies to every aspect of life.

After generous servings of pumpkin pie, it was time for Doug's pre-game nap. His routine is the same before every game. After the nap, he spent time preparing mentally for the opponent that night. This evening, it would be the Minnesota North Stars.

The official game program at the Capital Centre featured a full-color photograph of Doug, in the Caps' red, white and blue uniform, on the cover. His face was a picture of studied intensity: eyes focused and tongue hanging out as he stickhandled the puck.

The game that night was hard-fought. Late in the first period, Doug fed a pass from behind the Minnesota net to teammate Mike Gartner who was planted in the slot. Mike's shot into the upper left-hand corner of the net gave the Caps a 2-1 lead. But the team, struggling early in the season, couldn't hold on and settled for a 3-3 tie. In the last five minutes of regulation and the overtime, Doug took ten faceoffs in the Capitals' zone and won eight to help stave off the North Star attack.

After the game, Coach Murray was disappointed. "We should get the win at home," he said. Still it was early in the season and he remained optimistic about his team's potential. He reminded reporters that the previous year, the Caps had lost their first seven games, only to rebound and finish just three points behind the division champion Islanders.

About Doug, he said, "He's very competitive. He's willing to stick his nose in and be aggressive, and he plays hurt. He's top notch defensively and on faceoffs, and he uses his linemates extremely well."

Playing every game again this particular season, Doug wound up the year second only to Garry Unger for most consecutive games played in a career. In his quiet way, Doug was proving that it pays to play solid, fundamental hockey. "I feel God has given me the talent and the strength to maintain a career in hockey," he said with a humble smile. "As a Christian, whatever you do, it should be your very best." And for Doug Jarvis, that's very good indeed.

Glenn "Chico" Resch

6

GLENN "CHICO" RESCH

The uppermost level of the Byrne Meadowlands Arena is called the halo. Viewed from there by members of the media who peer down five stories to the ice, the players look more like toys than full-grown athletes.

Goaltender Glenn Resch, better known as "Chico," was perched in the halo along with two other teammates who were injured. Chico's career record against the evening's opponent, the Washington Capitals, was twelve wins and three ties in twenty one games, including four shutouts and a 1.82 goals-against average. But a pulled muscle in his shoulder prevented him from suiting up. Dressed in slacks, tie and a tweed sportscoat, Chico kept a shot chart, marking the location of every shot on goal and the number of the player who took the shot.

Two nights earlier, he had played a superb game in goal for the New Jersey Devils, only to lose a heartbreaker to Edmonton. The Oilers were gunning for another NHL record, this time for most games — fifteen — without a loss at the beginning of a season. The Devils had held them to a 2-2 tie with just 11 seconds left in regulation. Chico explained what happened then as he watched the game against Washington. "The faceoff was to my left and we won the draw. But Gretzky skated into the corner and both of our defensemen followed him, leaving Kurri alone in front of the net. Gretzky got the puck to him and he faked me, stepped around and threw the puck in the far corner of the net as I stretched out to try and stop him."

For a franchise that had played only two playoff games in its entire history, this was a heartbreaking loss. Few even remember that the team was born in Kansas City in 1974, moved to Colorado two years later, then moved again to New Jersey in 1982.

But bitter as the defeat was, it didn't take long for the veteran Chico to shake off the loss. "I don't know how long I was on my knees," he said about the Kurri goal. "Of course, the Oilers were celebrating, jumping all over each other. I was numb. We skated off the ice a few seconds later and I was really disappointed. Frustrated.

"When something like that happens, I like to talk about it. If you leave it overnight, you start thinking, 'What was my teammate thinking?' Or he may think, 'What was Chico doing?' I feel better if we can talk about it right then, and learn from it. Then you don't go to bed with it on your mind. Of course, we had to talk to the press. They came in about 15 minutes after the game. I tried to analyze it logically, not emotionally. I tried to give them an accurate description of what happened, yet also end it on a positive note.

"I guess I've learned it doesn't pay to dwell too long on a loss like that. If you can believe it, I've never had an official come in and say, 'O.K., because you're so disappointed, we're going to give you a break and change it.' It's over and you have to move on."

The New Jersey-Washington game ended with a flurry of activity in front of the New Jersey net in the final minute of overtime. But goalie Ron Low withstood the Washington attack to help New Jersey earn a 2-2 tie. As Chico went down to the locker room after the final horn, numerous fans greeted him. "Hi Chico!" "How you doing, Chico?" "We missed you tonight, Chico." It was clear proof that Glenn Resch is one of the most popular athletes in the New York area.

At thirty six, Resch already was the second oldest player in the league, having played goal for twelve seasons for the New York Islanders and the Colorado-New Jersey franchise. Earlier this season, he had become the twenty-sixth goalie to record two hundred victories in his career. He had represented both Team

Canada and Team USA in various international
competitions . . . Played in three all-star games . . . Won
the Bill Masterton Trophy for perseverence, sportsmanship
and dedication to hockey . . . Recorded twenty-six
shutouts . . . Won a Stanley Cup championship . . . Thus,
it was no surprise to see him enjoying the fruits of a
spectacular career and a reputation as a player who
cared about the fans.

After his obligatory appearance in the locker room,
Chico found his wife, Diane, and eleven-year-old daughter
Holly and headed for their cozy three-bedroom home in
Ridgewood, about a 25-minute drive from the Meadowlands
complex. "The *New York Times* called this one of the
two most livable communities in the metropolitan area,"
said Diane as the family ate bologna sandwiches. The
casual atmosphere immediately put a guest at ease.

Chico told why he had insisted on only a one-year
contract for this season, instead of the two-year deal
offered by the team. "I'm an endangered species," he
laughed. "Diane and I felt I wasn't as motivated last
season as I should have been. You don't want to do this,
but sometimes you think, What difference does it make
whether I play well and we lose 3-2, or I play just average
and we lose 5-2? I didn't want to end my career just
getting by and taking the money. A one-year contract
means I have to give my all. If it's my last year, I feel good,
and if the Lord wants me to play more, I can still sign for
another year. I needed that extra incentive."

The night was short, and the next morning Chico
drove 40 minutes to speak to a father-son breakfast at the

First Presbyterian Church of Whippany. He had slept only three and a half hours, sacrificing to put the finishing touches on his talk. A crowd of ninety men and boys filled two long tables in the church basement. It was the largest turnout ever, according to emcee Marshall Johnston, who is New Jersey's director of player personnel, and who had coached the team during its last year in Colorado.

"Glenn is the epitome of a role model," Johnston said in his introduction, "one we would be happy to have our sons and daughters follow."

Chico caused immediate laughter by saying, "I'd come to this church, too, if I heard a devil was going to speak!" A hush came over the hall as he began to relate some insights from his career. The wives and mothers who had served the breakfast came out of the kitchen to listen. "I used to think that playing in the NHL would be heaven. Then I played in New York and [against] Montreal and Boston, and it wasn't heaven. So I thought winning the Stanley Cup would be heaven. And in 1980, with the Islanders, I accomplished it. I remember not wanting to go to sleep that night, afraid the thrill of it would end. After a week, I realized it wasn't heaven, either."

Chico then described a personal odyssey in which he looked for things to provide happiness. He'd fulfilled all of his dreams. Made a lot of money. Received more praise than most people. Everything he thought should bring satisfaction only left him muttering the words of a Peggy Lee song — "Is that all there is?"

The goalie of the Islanders during their ascendance, "Chico" Resch has been between the pipes for more than 200 victories even though he is not now with a playoff contender.

The change came at a conference for professional athletes. He attended because a well-known football player had called a similar conference the greatest experience of his life. "I knew this player had enjoyed many thrills in football, so I had to see what was so special." There, Chico experienced the love of Christian athletes, and the One who gives that love, Jesus Christ.

Chico admits he was a skeptic at first, that he had to check out the facts about Christ. He found them to be overwhelming. The evidence about Christ's life was extensive. The death of Jesus Christ, His burial, and His resurrection three days later were among the most established facts of history. "Once I saw all that, I realized my decision was made." At the conference, Chico thanked God for the sacrifice that Christ made to pay for his sins, and he began a relationship with Him.

"Since then, it's been a process of growth," Chico said as he reached the conclusion to his message. "God has shown me that His playbook is the Bible. I think this is the greatest news I could ever share, and that's why I was willing to get up at 6:30 in the morning on my day off."

During the question and answer session, a boy asked how Resch got his nickname. "When I was a rookie with the Islanders," he said, "I lived in a building with mostly Spanish-speaking people. One of them often drove me to practice, and he was always calling to me, 'Hey, Chico!' It caught on."

Another fan wanted to know Chico's evaluation of Wayne Gretzky. "There's no simple explanation for why he's so great. You would think that the fastest skater or the guy with the hardest shot would have all the advantages. He doesn't have either, but he uses his head. He sees things no one else sees. Sure, he has a lot of talent, but he works hard and doesn't waste it."

It wasn't a complete day off for Chico. After the breakfast, he drove to the team's training complex and changed into a sweat suit. He ran three miles in freezing rain, then received treatment from the trainer for his ailing shoulder.

That afternoon, he relaxed by watching television in his upstairs den — the New York Jets were struggling against the Indianapolis Colts. With the sound turned down, he surprised his guest by admitting that as a youngster, he was very shy. It was hard to believe that such a personable, outgoing man should ever have considered himself, as Chico states it, "a borderline nerd."

"I was small as a kid — I still am small — and I wasn't a good skater. In pickup games, the other kids always made me play goal because no one else wanted to play goal."

The problem was that he was afraid to initiate conversation with anyone besides his family and closest friends. That trend continued during his first two years in the NHL, though fans didn't realize it because he was often quoted in the press. He was comfortable when someone approached and asked a question, but he was afraid to get close to anyone.

Two events helped correct that. One occurred while he was a member of Team Canada in 1976. "I was so in awe of my teammates that I wanted to ask for their autographs. I was so intimidated, that the few times I even said anything, I felt stupid. So I kept my mouth shut. Then one day, a player said in front of everyone, 'I've heard you are supposed to be such a talker, yet I haven't heard you say two words. Can't you say anything?' " Glenn was crushed, yet it made him think. He wanted to be a team player. He wanted to be accepted. To do that, he decided, he would have to take some risks and work at it.

The most important factor was his commitment to Christ. "I realized that everything God has created is for our enjoyment. He created people and put us all together, and He wants us to enjoy each other. That's when I really began to change."

The transformation wasn't immediate. There were mistakes — talking too quickly, saying things better left unsaid, being insensitive. But the more he practiced reaching out, the more comfortable he felt with people. Often it was fun. He found he could help others feel significant. He went out of his way to meet the maintenance and concession workers in every arena in the league and he now knows many on a first-name basis.

Not everyone responds to his warmth, but that doesn't deter him. "I used to take it personally when I was rejected. But you don't know what kind of a day a person is having. Or perhaps he is nervous when you reach out to him, and he doesn't know how to respond.

In hockey, if you get a chance for a breakaway and the goalie stops you, you don't say you never want another breakaway. You try again the next time. So if a person doesn't respond to me, I try again another day."

He has some simple techniques for making people feel comfortable. "If you want people to like you, don't tell them how great you are. Then they feel they have to put you down. Instead build them up, and they'll often build you up, too. The best thing you can do is ask a person something you know he has an answer for. Or say something that will make him feel good.

"Generally people don't feel that they're important. I think that's one thing Christ really wants us to focus on. You *are* important. You have a lot of worth. God created you — that says a lot right there. If you were worth making, then He thinks you're good. That's really why I'm not insecure any more."

Chico believes God has used him to reach out to others for Christ. Because of his warm personality and sincere interest in people, he has organized chapel services for his teammates while in New York and Colorado, and presently holds a Bible study for some of his New Jersey teammates. In the summer, he reaches out to youngsters through the Christian Athlete hockey camp program.

After spending time with Chico Resch, you can't help but notice that his personality affects you. Sure, he is an outstanding player. He's been one of the NHL's better goalies for years. But when you're with him, you don't think of him as a star. He looks at you. He listens. He cares. Long after his career is over and his statistics are forgotten, Chico will be remembered — because he gave people some of the love that he receives from God.

Doug Smail

7
DOUG SMAIL
and
LAURIE BOSCHMAN

The entry of the Winnipeg Jets in the National
Hockey League was considered a joke by some.
It didn't matter that they'd been one of the
premier teams in the World Hockey Association and
winner of its final Avco Cup championship. One NHL
executive expressed this feeling when he said, "Winnipeg?
What do we want a whistle-stop cow town like that in
the league for?"

When the Jets were assimilated into the NHL in 1979,
it didn't help that they'd lost several key players,

including Anders Hedberg, Ulf Nilsson, and Bobby Hull. That year they tied the Colorado Rockies for the worst record in the league. It was downhill from there. They won a grand total of nine games during the 1980-81 season, and set a record for futility by going thirty straight games without a win. Doug Smail was a member of that team and he never wants to be embarrassed like that again.

Laurie Boschman was a more recent import to the Jets, but like Smail, he knows what it's like to be ridiculed. While playing with another team, he was the object of public scorn by a frustrated owner. His beliefs were held up for examination by the press. People questioned his ability to play tough, hard-nosed hockey while maintaining a commitment to God.

Perhaps their past was one reason Doug Smail and Laurie Boschman became such close friends. They'd suffered through intense trials and survived to become respected players. Smail, a lightning quick left winger, and Boschman, a tenacious center, were now teammates on a Winnipeg Jets team that had finally gained respect in the NHL. Currently, they occupied third place in the Smythe Division, only two points behind Calgary. They'd won more games than they'd lost, despite a rough stretch during the Christmas season when they'd dropped eight of ten games.

The fast-skating pair had just helped the Jets pummel the Vancouver Canucks for the team's third straight win. Laurie had contributed an assist on a rink-long rush that ended with a pass to Perry Turnbull for an easy score. Doug had just missed an assist in a short-handed situation when Tom Steen hit the post. It was a satisfying win, only the third ever for the Jets in Vancouver's Pacific Coliseum.

After a short drive through Vancouver's fog shrouded streets, the two friends found an all-night diner, and we all settled down for a long talk.

Doug, a small man with a shock of wavy brown hair and a mustache, came to the Jets in 1980 after a stellar collegiate career at the University of North Dakota. While at North Dakota, he experienced a national championship and won the NCAA most valuable player award. Laurie, three inches taller but looking thinner than his 185 pounds would suggest, joined the Jets near the end of the 82-83 season. This was his third NHL team and he finally was coming into his own as an all-around player. His 28 goals the year before doubled his previous season's best. "I'm more confident," he admitted. "I know my role now."

Laurie was the more talkative and was eager to explain how the Christian faith they share has drawn them together. "Doug and I have talked about how loosely some people use the term Christian. I figured I was a Christian because I went to church and didn't do bad things. But it's more than that, and it wasn't until I received Christ that I understood. I think some of the guys expect us to be overhuman. They tease us, but they're always watching."

Doug expanded on that thought, talking softly against the noise of dishes clattering in the background. "There's an interest on this team, a desire to know where we're coming from."

These committed Christian players endure a certain amount of clubhouse joking, and the two forwards aren't afraid to kid back. But they agree that their teammates are a great bunch of guys. "I think we fit in quite well," said Laurie. "We play the game as hard as we can, and the guys know that, and they respect the stand we've taken."

Doug agrees. "We're here to play hockey, not bang guys over the head with Bibles. If we have the chance to share [the gospel], we're more than willing. But right now, this is our career, a way to provide a living for our families." (Doug's family consisted of himself and his wife Lisa, and Laurie was looking forward to getting married at the end of the season.)

The impact of Christian players on the team is a significant one, partly because Laurie's faith became an issue of national concern in Canada while he was with the Toronto Maple Leafs. The swift center had been a first round draft pick of the Leafs following an outstanding junior career with the Brandon Wheat Kings. During his rookie year, teammate Ron Ellis organized Sunday chapel services for the Leafs. After the final service of the season, Laurie committed his life to Christ with the help of speaker Mel Stevens who runs the Christian Teen Ranch in Toronto.

It seemed that Laurie's problems started soon after that. He spent a week in the minors the next year,

Since Laurie Boschman joined the Jets he has doubled his goal production to an average of 30 goals a year.

suffered blood poisoning, and contracted mononucleosis. The mono sapped his strength and affected his performance on the ice. Team owner Harold Ballard blasted his player in a television interview after a loss to the Rangers in New York, saying that he was going to trade Laurie because he had too much religion on his mind.

"I didn't know what had happened," Laurie says now of the incident. "Darryl Sittler [the Leafs' captain] told me about it the next day. Of course, the press interviewed me. My teammates were very supportive. They had seen me before, when I wasn't a Christian. I worked as hard or harder, and I was a better person off the ice. They knew being a Christian didn't make me a weak-kneed wimp."

Despite that support, the publicity of the story led to a trade with Edmonton midway through that season. Doug was aware of the story and like most players, "I wrote it off as a bad rap. Laurie has proved Ballard totally wrong. If people on other teams thought it was something serious, they wouldn't have traded for him."

Doug can relate to his teammate's adversity. During his first season, in addition to the embarrassment of the team's record, he broke his jaw twice and was also sidelined by a blood clot in his chest. He played only thirty of the team's eighty games. "God used those times to slow me down. In college, my closest friends had also accepted Christ, but in Winnipeg, I had no Christian fellowship. I didn't find a church, so my spiritual life began eroding. I compromised on some things and engaged in some questionable activities. God used those setbacks to show me that I can't make it on my own."

Listening to these two men might cause one to think that it's dangerous to become a Christian. Doug disagreed. "These things are going to happen whether you're a believer in Jesus Christ or not. If you're walking down the sidewalk and a car drives through a puddle and splashes you, that doesn't happen because you're a Christian. However, if I hadn't accepted Jesus Christ, I don't think I would have been able to handle those circumstances. That's what knowing Christ has shown me. I've got Someone to help me through these problems."

Our discussion ended at 1:30 in the morning and resumed in the hotel coffee shop eight hours later. The Jets' duo talked about how God had affected their social lives. "It took about five months before the reality of my commitment began to sink in," said Laurie over a bowl of oatmeal. "Eventually, I stopped drinking altogether. My sister was killed in a car accident by someone who was drinking. The Holy Spirit convicted me that I don't need it, so I've stopped completely. And I honestly don't miss it."

Doug admitted his lifestyle was similar in many respects. In high school, he experimented with drugs and stopped only after his father presented him with some facts, leaving the decision to him. "I just started drinking more," he said. "I changed only after I thought of it in terms of my relationship with Jesus Christ. Like 'Bosch' says, when the Holy Spirit lays something on you, you reach the point where you will act on it. I feel we

Doug Smail joined the Winnipeg Jets after being named the NCAA's Most Valuable Player in the 1979-80 season.

should live an exemplary life in obedience to what God is saying." That doesn't mean he won't go out with the players, but he is willing to drink orange juice while others drink alcohol.

An exemplary lifestyle isn't easy, and both players admit they fail at times. Doug told about how he recently lost his temper in practice and the coach had to separate him from another player. "No one had to tell me I blew it. The next morning I knew I had to apologize. I went over to do that, and the other guy apologized to me first. Then I apologized to him. That's the kind of people we're working with. We're a team."

That example perhaps shows how much these two players have changed. Doug doesn't hesitate to say that he might well have ignored his loss of temper a few years ago. He was, by his admission, selfish, concerned only about himself and his hockey career.

Hockey is a contact sport, and the two players want to play as hard as they can within the rules. They admit that emotions frequently run high and that it's not easy to control those emotions. Yet they don't consider letting up. Doug says that he often stays up until four in the morning after a game, reviewing every play in his mind, trying to learn how he could have done better.

"There's no worse feeling than when you know that you didn't give 100 percent," said Laurie. "We strive to give our very best. Then, no matter whether we win or lose, we're at peace."

The other players in the restaurant began moving to the team bus which would transport them to practice.

Doug commented that he enjoys every aspect of his work and looks forward to practice. Both Doug and Laurie enjoy their relationship as Christians and compare it to the camaraderie of a team. "The great thing about a team sport is that we back each other up," Laurie added. "We have a common bond."

"There's an unspoken confidence," said Doug of his friendship with Laurie. "We can share things we normally wouldn't share with others. If you're mentally tired, if you're not ready for a game, you can't share those things with your other teammates. But Laurie and I help each other give that 100 percent."

As they walked through the hotel lobby toward the bus, Doug wanted to clarify that their faith means more than just attending church. Both were involved in church activities long before they understood what it meant to be related to Jesus Christ. "Christianity is a choice," said Doug. "An ever-after choice. I want people to see it's a relationship with Jesus Christ, not belief in a religion."

Laurie emphasized that point as we parted. "Look how Christ brings us together. We can talk openly and we feel uplifted. That's why it's so great to be a Christian; you have so much in common with fellow Christians!"

Ed Kea

8

ED KEA

Ed Kea is tall, three inches above six feet, with clearly defined muscles bulging from his arms and chest. But physical strength could not help him tackle the problem he faced. He tried to relax on the couch as he studied the Trivial Pursuit question. His wife, Jennifer, looked over his shoulder as he read haltingly. "What ba . . . bad . . . b . . . "

"Balding," Jennifer coached, like the English teacher she once was.

"What balding defenseman toy . . ."

"Toiled."

". . . toiled on the Dee . . . Dee . . . "

"Detroit."

"Detroit Red Wings blue line from . . . 19 . . . 1964 to 1973?"

"That's good. Can you answer the question?"

There was a long silence as Ed studied the card, perhaps wishing he could see through to the answer on the other side. Maybe he knew the player personally but couldn't recall his name. Jennifer explained that Ed enjoyed playing the sports version of this game, and usually did well on the hockey questions. But today, the answers came slowly. Finally he just shook his head and Jennifer turned the card over to reveal the answer: Gary Bergman.

Glance at Ed Kea and you will think he could strap on the skates and quickly resume the NHL career that saw him become one of the league's better defensemen. But Ed will never play hockey again. He is fortunate to be alive, much less walking and talking.

It's amazing that Ed Kea even made it to the NHL. He was the second youngest of fourteen children in a family that immigrated to Canada from Holland. When he wasn't working on the family farm near Collingwood, Ontario, he was usually playing soccer. He did not play organized hockey until the age of eighteen when he joined a Junior C club. He survived five years in the minor leagues before joining the Atlanta Flames in 1974 at the age of twenty-five.

Ed enjoyed five stellar seasons with the Flames and another four with the St. Louis Blues, 583 games in all.

He was a solid defenseman who frequently led his team in the +/- category that compares the number of goals scored and allowed while a player is actually on the ice. But it all came to a sudden and unexpected end in Salt Lake City.

Jennifer did most of the talking as she and Ed reviewed the story of the event in Salt Lake that changed their lives. The afternoon sun filtered softly through the curtains of their suburban St. Louis home to give a 19th-century feel to the antique-filled house. The coffee table was a Civil War rifle box. One end table was an old Canadian Barrack box; the other a butcher block. Visible in the foyer was an original milk can from the Kea dairy.

"Ed wasn't playing much in home games," Jennifer said concerning her husband's ninth NHL season. "He was thirty five, and the Blues were giving more playing time to some of their younger defensemen. He told management that if they weren't going to play him, he wanted to be traded."

Soon after that, Ed was sent to the Blues' minor league team in Salt Lake City. He played exceptionally well, and after four games, General Manager Emile Francis recalled him as the Blues prepared for the playoffs. But the Salt Lake team wanted to use him for one more game before he flew back to St. Louis the next day.

The Salt Lake City Eagles were playing Tulsa that fateful night in March of 1983. Kea was helping to kill a penalty as he scooped up a loose puck and skated behind the Tulsa net. He never saw George McPhee approaching at full speed from the right. It was a legal check. The left winger's shoulder met Ed's chest and sent him flying into the boards. The force of his head crashing into the boards propelled him face-first onto the ice, breaking his nose and leaving him unconscious. Later, Emile Francis said that he'd never seen such a hard check.

Jennifer received the news late that night. "It seems like a hundred years ago now," she says. "I'd fallen asleep watching television. The neurosurgeon called and told me Ed was in a semi-coma, with an injury to the side of the brain that controls speech. I was only half awake, so I don't think it really registered."

Sensing she would need a good night's rest, Jennifer went back to sleep. The next day she made arrangements for their four children, ages one, three, six and nine. No one was too worried; Ed had suffered numerous injuries during his career.

The love that this couple shares is evident as they talk. Jennifer was a young schoolteacher from Toronto when they first met — a herd of the Keas' cattle had surrounded her car in the middle of the roadway. Ed smiles at the memory. "After that I made sure there were some cows in the road about the time she was driving to work." They married while Ed was playing minor league hockey. Theirs is a deep love, molded by their mutual Christian commitment and the fact that they are also best friends. "We'd rather be with each other than anyone else," says Jennifer.

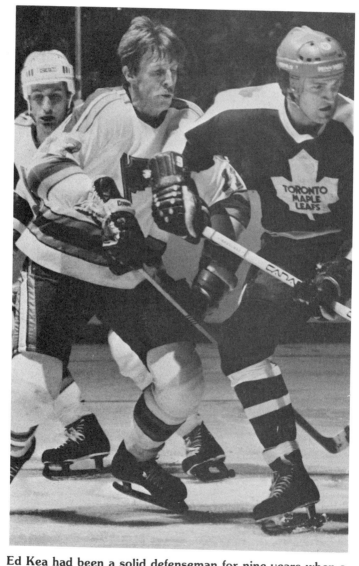

Ed Kea had been a solid defenseman for nine years when a head injury suddenly halted his career.

That love faced its stiffest test when Jennifer entered the intensive care unit of Holy Cross Hospital in Salt Lake City. "He looked like he'd been run over by a truck. Both eyes were black. Blood on his head had hardened. He was unconscious, yet his body did move when stimulated."

That changed within the next forty eight hours as Ed drifted into a coma. A staff person asked Jennifer if she wanted last rites said for her husband, and if she was ready to make "arrangements" for a funeral. Finally the doctor informed her that the pressure on Ed's brain was so great that only surgery could save his life. There was a 50 percent chance it would not succeed.

At that point, despite the many people who were coming by the hospital to comfort Jennifer, the only place for her to turn to was God. "I remember thinking that I knew Ed was ready to go to heaven. He'd talked a lot about heaven and what a great place it would be. Though I didn't want to go through it, I knew God would provide whatever I needed if Ed died. I prayed and told God that if I had my "druthers," I'd rather Ed stayed and helped me raise those four kids. After that prayer, I had a perfect peace. There was nothing more I could do; I'd passed the ball into the Lord's court."

Ed was on the operating table for six and a half hours as doctors cut open his skull to release the pressure. Afterward, Jennifer described him as looking like Frankenstein. "His head was shaved and they put staples in it where the incision was made."

For ten long days, Ed remained in a coma. Jennifer spent most of her waking hours by his side, praying, reading him the many cards and letters that came from around the country, telling him about their children, and reading to him from the Bible. Nurses warned her to expect a different person when he "woke up," one with no moral values, spewing forth vulgar language. But when that day came, Ed had a smile and a wink for his wife, and puckered his lips for a kiss.

Ed doesn't remember anything of the ordeal. "I don't remember the last two games," he says. "I think it was five weeks before I remembered something. I was at the house here in St. Louis. Two of my sisters were here. Aggie and Nellie."

Ed was flown home on a private jet by the owner of the Blues. On his family's first visit to the hospital, Ed did not seem to recognize all his children. He was just a skeleton of his once-healthy self, having lost more than thirty pounds. It was early April before he uttered his first words, and those early words were almost exclusively about Jesus Christ. His face radiated as he told about how Christ stood next to him through the ordeal. Though unable to express himself fluently, he clearly communicated his deep love for God.

By the time we talked in the Kea home, more than twenty months had passed since the accident and the incident had been forgotten by many hockey fans. Recovery was slow, and it may never be complete. At first, Ed had to hang on to his wife in order to jog around the block. Now he could walk or jog the two miles to therapy three times a week. The right half of the vision in each eye was gone, which meant he could not drive. But the main problem was his speech. "I know what things are," he explained, "but I can't say the right words." His wife compared it to a person who speaks German trying to communicate with someone who knows only English.

Much of Ed's therapy has consisted of looking at pictures and trying to match the corresponding name to that picture. Often, Jennifer felt like a grade school teacher having to instruct Ed on the most basic concepts. Sometimes the same lesson had to be repeated several times.

The progress was slow, and there were periodic setbacks. In recent weeks, Ed had experienced depression, a side-effect of his medicine. Twice, he'd suffered epileptic-type seizures. But the hardest problems were social. "Ed gets into speech patterns where he reproduces the same conversation with everybody," Jennifer explained. "It's as if he has these mini-cassettes of what he thinks is appropriate speech."

Before the accident, Ed was a quiet, almost shy person. Since the accident, there have been times when he has overreacted, forgetting basic social practices most of us take for granted. "Ed's still the same sweet person," says Jennifer. "But he's had an injury. If I don't tell him what he does wrong, there is no way he can ever correct it." She emphasized that Ed is not brain-damaged, which connotes permanency. Rather he has suffered an injury and there is hope for an eventual recovery.

Both Ed and Jennifer work at maintaining an upbeat approach to the situation. Jennifer calls it uphill thinking. "You can go on a downhill slide with negative thinking, thinking that this is as good as Ed is going to get. Or you can think uphill with the hope that is in Christ, concentrating on His promises. I've learned to be thankful for where we are right now."

Despite the many problems they face, Jennifer believes that the God who has taken such good care of them will continue to do so. "In Psalm 37 we read, 'I have been young, and now am old; but I have not seen the righteous forsaken, or his descendants begging bread.' In Philippians, Paul writes, 'My God shall supply all your needs according to His riches in glory in Christ Jesus.' "

After the injury, a lot of publicity was given to the fact that Ed never played with a helmet. He was one of the few remaining holdouts, claiming that the resulting perspiration hindered his vision. But no one knows if a helmet would have reduced the severity of the injury. Some feel that the initial force of his head against the boards would probably have knocked his helmet off, and it certainly would not have helped when his face hit the ice. Nevertheless, three teammates as well as several others in the NHL who had not worn helmets before started wearing them as a result of his accident.

Ed's injury is not unique. It happens frequently in car accidents. His was different only because it took place in a professional hockey game. Thus, the Keas hope their story will be one of encouragement to the many families who suffer silently.

Watching the Kea family, you are impressed that the force that holds them together is love — love for God and love for each other. "Love is not a feeling. It's a commitment," Jennifer explains. "It's a decision. When we were married, we made vows to each other. We would love each other for better or for worse, in sickness and in health. Love is not just for the good times. I often complain about my weight, and Ed says he'll trade problems with me. I know I wouldn't want to have his problem. I don't think I'd have enough self-confidence to handle it. But I'm going to try to help him handle it."

Ed smiled as his wife talked. "The Lord knows what she can take, and the Lord knows what I can take."

"Right! Ed says he doesn't remember all the Scripture he memorized. But he just quoted 1 Corinthians 10:13." Jennifer was quiet for a moment and from the street came the sounds of children arriving home from school. "Maybe Ed doesn't remember a lot of the Bible, but he knows the God of the Bible. He's a Christ-like man. A lot of things have changed. He trips and falls sometimes. He has some depression. He can't see well. But he still has that tender heart. It would be easy for us to feel sorry for ourselves. There is a lot of stress. But we keep thinking of God's encouragement for us to cast our cares on Him, because He cares for us. I'm thankful that's true."

Mark Osborne

9

MARK OSBORNE

Excitement and energy from the crowd of more than seventeen thousand New Yorkers surged throughout Madison Square Garden and captivated the players. The National Anthem was not even half completed when fans began whistling and clapping, then cheering. The roar grew until the final strains of music were completely engulfed by the noise.

The decibel level in Madison Square Garden is perhaps the highest in the National Hockey League, and it seems to peak for games between the Rangers and the New York Islanders. Ever since J.P. Parise scored 11 seconds into overtime to give the three-year-old Islanders a shocking 2-1 playoff series win over the Rangers in 1975, games between these two teams have been among the NHL's most hotly contested. Twice this season, the Rangers had scored incredible come-from-behind victories over their cross-town rivals. Twice, the Islanders had crushed the team from Manhattan like a big bully who rules a grade school playground.

For Mark Osborne, tonight's game meant more than a chance to compete against the four-time Stanley Cup champions. It was the Rangers' fifty-eighth regular season game, yet this was Mark's first appearance of the year in uniform. Two severely pulled muscles had kept him sidelined until now.

The season had been a major disappointment not only for Mark but also for the Rangers. The team led the league in man-games lost to injury — nearly four hundred. The list was gruesome. Don Maloney and Mark Pavelich, broken ankles. Anders Hedberg, eye injury. Ron Greschner, separated shoulder. Tom Laidlaw, spleen removed. Like Mark, all were veterans and their injuries crippled a team that one year before had recorded forty-two wins, fourth best in the history of the franchise that has not won a Stanley Cup since 1940.

In the midst of this trying season, Coach Herb Brooks was fired and replaced by General manager Craig Patrick. Craig's heritage was a link to great Ranger teams of the past since both his father and uncle had coached and each had served as general manager. Despite a recent seven-game road trip that produced six losses and a tie, the team seemed to relax under new leadership.

Two nights before this game, the Rangers had exploded for eight goals to defeat Edmonton, 8-7. The offense continued rolling this evening. Mark was teamed on a line with George McPhee and Bob Brooke, both of whom also had spent time on the injured squad. McPhee and Brooke scored within 2:15 as part of a five-goal second period explosion. The fans, who so readily jeered when their Rangers floundered, were ecstatic. Their involvement reached a feverish pitch at the end of the second period when the two teams engaged in a brawl that saw three players from each side, including both goalies, ejected with game misconducts. Final score: Rangers 9, Islanders 3.

Mark was exhilarated after the contest. "You can't help but get emotionally involved for a game like this," he said. "It's been so long for me, I felt a little lost out there for the first period or two. I thought if I could just go out tonight and hit somebody, do some forechecking, create some opportunities . . . That's all I was trying to do."

That he'd played and contributed to a win meant a great deal. "I've been through so much, my hopes have gone up and down so many times, that I wondered if I'd ever play this year. I was surprised — I actually had a lot more ice time than I expected tonight. My body's sore, but to tell you the truth, it feels good!"

Mark was nearly recovered two nights later as he relaxed in his condominium twenty miles north of Manhattan. The quiet, wooded development is located close to the team's practice facility near the Connecticut border, and it provides a peaceful atmosphere compared to the hectic pace of Manhattan.

With the stereo tuned to an easy-listening FM music station, Mark attacked a pile of bills that had accumulated during a two-week road trip. Patrick had invited Mark and several other injured players to travel with the squad, and as a result, Mark began to feel a part of the team for the first time all year, making the transition to playing much easier.

The 6'2" left winger talked freely about the frustrations of the season. "Our team had a really good year last year, and we were looking forward to good things this season. But when the team struggled, and I wasn't able to participate, it was very frustrating."

Mark's problems began during final workouts prior to training camp when he strained his right hip flexor muscle. "That's the muscle you use to walk up stairs, and when you skate," he explained. "You even use it when driving, when you lift your leg to move your foot between the brake and accelerator pedals."

At first, any leg exercise aggravated the injury. Team trainers suggested several forms of treatment, but nothing seemed to work except complete rest of the injured area. To maintain some conditioning, Mark swam and exercised his upper body.

For an athlete who had missed only seven games in his first three seasons — the result of a bad case of flu — the injury was hard to accept. He'd had a pin

Mark Osborne has been one of the rising young stars on the New York Ranger team.

placed in the hip five years earlier, and doctors thought perhaps this injury was the result of improper rehabilitation.

Then in December, shortly before Mark was due to return to the lineup, the left hip began hurting. It was his left hip flexor, and the process of rest and rehabilitation had to be repeated.

"This wasn't the type of injury where I could set a time limit," Mark said. "Every time I thought I was going to play, I'd be disappointed again. The only thing that really kept me going was encouragement from my Christian friends and my own relationship with God. This drew me closer to Him, and I'm confident God let it happen for a purpose."

Little had gone wrong in Mark's life before this year. He'd grown up in Toronto and played junior hockey in Niagara Falls. His only time in the minor leagues was a playoff appearance for Adirondack of the American Hockey League immediately following his final season of junior hockey. He was a second-round draft choice of the Detroit Red Wings in 1980 and led the Wings in scoring as a rookie. After two solid seasons in Detroit, he was traded to the Rangers where he was the team's hottest scorer during the final part of the 83-84 season, scoring four game-winning goals, including two in overtime.

Perhaps the hardest job for an injured player is watching the games from the stands. Mark said the fans were good to him, but he grew tired of answering the question, "When will you be back?" For months, it seemed like the answer was always, "Just two more weeks."

"I've learned a lot about myself," he said as he leaned on his kitchen counter. "It's been humbling, yet it's forced me to trust God."

One highlight that emerged from Mark's injury-riddled season is an answer to his off-season prayer. For three seasons, he had not had a teammate with whom he could enjoy Christian fellowship. In December, one of his Ranger teammates, after many months of questioning, trusted Jesus Christ to be his Savior. "That made my year," he said. "That's life's highest purpose."

Mark grew up in a home where Christian principles were practiced, but he didn't make a personal commitment to Christ until he was fourteen years old. "It happened when my uncle died. That was the first time I'd been exposed to death. Shortly after that, I was listening to the Sunday morning sermon — that was unusual for me — and I realized that I believed in God and Jesus Christ. I even believed that He came down from heaven, died on a cross and rose again from the dead. But it wasn't personal. That morning I confessed my sins and asked Jesus Christ to come into my heart."

While the decision was sincere, Mark doesn't feel he started to grow spiritually until he left home to play junior hockey. Homesick and lonely, trying to be a Christian in the midst of negative peer pressure, he had to lean on God. "I wanted to be part of the team, but I wasn't going to give up my moral convictions. That's the way it still is for me."

That strength of character can be tested in a city like New York. Mark doesn't like everything about the city, but it does offer a lot for a young person. He is charged by the emotional energy that comes from the people, yet also realizes the need to draw away at times, to stay close to his church, to read the Bible, to be quiet.

As a result, Mark has lost the cockiness that characterized him as a teenager. Some of it is maturity. But mostly it is due to his growth in Christ. "Through the years, I've learned more about myself by knowing God. I've learned to think of others as more important than myself. The Bible tells us not to be selfish but to have an attitude like Jesus Christ. He was God, but He humbled Himself, became a man, and died for us. What I try to do is take the focus off me and draw it to Christ."

One way he does that is through Christian Athlete Hockey Camps in the summer. He participates in two or three week-long camps each year, teaching youngsters the game and sharing with them his faith in Christ. The camps are run by Hockey Ministries International under the leadership of Don Liesemer, a former professional hockey player in the Montreal organization.

Mark's face lights up as he thinks about the kids he's worked with. "There was a boy in New Brunswick — his parents were separated, his dad was an alcoholic. It was exciting to watch God break down his barriers as we prayed together and he received Christ. I think another highlight is when you come back after a year and you see how the kids have grown. That's a big encouragement to me, seeing God change people's lives. The camps also give me a chance to get to know other Christian players in the league, and I've been encouraged by Don's life, by how close he is to God. He's been an example and a teacher to me."

God has changed Mark's life, and one evidence of that was his perspective now that he was playing hockey again after a ten-month layoff. "God taught me to be patient during the past few months, especially as I got close to playing. As an athlete, you get anxious to perform and sometimes you get things out of focus. God has put things into focus for me."

Jean Pronovost

10

OVERTIME
Experience Your Own Personal Breakaway
by Jean Pronovost

Hockey is a great sport, one that has been a major part of my life. I grew up in a hockey family, and for twenty years my older brother Marcel was an all-star quality defenseman in the National Hockey league. Then I played fourteen seasons in the NHL and scored 391 goals in my career. When it comes to hockey, I certainly have enjoyed a lot of thrills.

When people ask me what my greatest moment was, my answer often surprises them. They expect me to talk about scoring 52 goals for Pittsburgh during the 1975-76 season. Scoring 50 goals in one season was a great personal achievement, but when I finally reached it, the thrill of that accomplishment lasted only a short time.

Without a doubt, my greatest experience, not only in hockey but in my entire life, occurred during the 1978-79 season when I experienced my own spiritual breakaway.

I hope you have enjoyed reading the stories in this book. The purpose of this last chapter is to explain how you, too, can experience a spiritual breakaway. To do that, I would like to point you to the Bible, where God gives us instructions for life.

Perhaps you're wondering just what a spiritual breakaway is. **First of all, it is a breakaway from sin.** Jesus said, "Everyone who commits sin is the slave of sin" (John 8:34). It's a fact that everyone has sinned and God says the penalty for sin is death. That means eternal separation from God in a place called hell.

Do you know what it means to be condemned? Former Boston Bruin Dave Forbes has a better understanding than most of us. You may remember that in 1974, he became the first professional athlete in North America to be tried in a court of law for an act of aggression during an athletic contest. The trial itself lasted ten days and ended in a hung jury.

If Dave had been convicted, he would have had to serve at least three years in jail. It was a tremendous

Jean Pronovost has scored 391 goals over a fourteen-season career in the NHL.

relief for him when he was allowed to resume his hockey career. But Dave's greatest moment came two years later, when he surrendered to Jesus Christ. That's when he was cleared of *all* the sins he'd ever committed. Unlike those who refuse to accept Christ, Dave would now not have to face the sentence of hell.

Second, a spiritual breakaway is a breakaway to fulfillment, purpose and eternal life in Christ.

Did you notice how many of the hockey players in this book said that their success in hockey did not give them lasting satisfaction? It's true that many accomplishments give us momentary enjoyment, but we always desire more. Jesus Christ said, "I came that they might have life, and might have it abundantly" (John 10:10).

People who are committed to Jesus Christ understand what it means to live a fulfilled life. The reason is that life does not end when we die. Jesus Christ explains, "Truly, truly, I say to you, he who hears My word, and believes Him who sent me, has eternal life, and does not come into judgment, but has passed out of death into life" (John 5:24). I can tell you from personal experience that I get far more lasting enjoyment out of seeing other people come to faith in Christ than I did from scoring goals in the National Hockey League.

Third, a spiritual breakaway is made possible by God's Son, who paid the price for our sins.

One of the Bible writers, the apostle Paul, explains: "For I delivered to you as of first importance what I also received, that Christ died for our sins according to the Scriptures, and that He was buried, and that He was raised on the third day according to the Scriptures, and that He appeared to Cephas, then to the twelve. After that He appeared to more than five hundred brethren at one time" (1 Corinthians 15:3-5).

The incredible message of the Bible is that God so loved you and me that He sent His Son, Jesus Christ, to take the punishment for our sins. Jesus Christ says that He is the only way to God, and the reason is that God placed all of our sins on Him when He died on the cross. His resurrection was proof that He is God's Son and that He really has the power to unite us with God.

Finally, a spiritual breakaway can be experienced by acknowledging that you are a sinner and receiving, by faith, God's free gift of salvation.

Paul Henderson achieved a unique thrill by scoring the winning goal in the final minute of play to give Canada the victory in their first-ever series against the Russians in 1972. That achievement — and two other game-winning goals in that series — made Paul a national hero, but they didn't bring him lasting satisfaction. He began a search for a deeper, spiritual side to life. In 1975, he found it in the person of Jesus Christ. His breakaway occurred through a prayer of faith. It wasn't long or profound. "I simply said, 'Lord Jesus, I want to change, but I can't change myself. I admit I'm a sinner. Thank You for dying for me. I ask You to come into my life. Amen.' "

This is the most important part of this book, for at this moment you can experience your own spiritual breakaway if you're ready. You can do it through prayer, a prayer as simple as the one Paul Henderson prayed. If you sincerely mean it, God will hear you. Your prayer should include the following thoughts:

(1)   Admit you are a sinner.

(2)   Thank God for sending His divine Son, Jesus Christ, to pay the penalty for your sin by dying on the cross and then rising from the dead.

(3)   Accept His forgiveness for your sins.

(4)   Invite Jesus Christ to come into your life and make you a new person.

Why don't you take a minute right now to pray this prayer in your own words?

                              *   *   *

Did you sincerely pray these thoughts to God? If you did, Jesus Christ came into your life. You may or may not feel any different at this moment. But that doesn't matter because your prayer is based on what God says, not on how you feel. However, if you did trust Christ to be your personal Savior, your life will begin to change.

It is important that you tell someone what has happened. The apostle Paul writes, "If you confess with your mouth Jesus as Lord, and believe in your heart that God raised Him from the dead, you shall be saved;

for with the heart man believes, resulting in righteousness, and with the mouth he confesses, resulting in salvation" (Romans 10:9, 10).

One of the main changes in my life is the love I have. I thought I loved my family before, but I realize now I was really quite selfish. God has given me a new love that makes me willing to stop thinking only about myself and to be more concerned about others.

God will change your life, but it won't happen overnight. Let me suggest three things that will help you walk with God:

(1)   Spend some time every day reading the Bible. The Bible is God speaking to us. If you don't know where to start, begin by reading the Gospel of John in the New Testament. You may have noticed that I quoted several verses from it in this chapter.

(2)   Take time to pray every day. Prayer is simply talking with God, just as you would talk with your best friend. You could start by thanking Jesus Christ for coming into your life. You might also ask God to teach you as you read from the Bible, and to cause you to be more willing to obey what He tells you to do.

(3)   If you are not attending church, start going every Sunday. You should choose a church which teaches the Bible. Attending church will give you an opportunity to meet with other believers, and you can encourage each other to grow in faith.

If you have given your life to Jesus Christ as a result of reading this book, or if you have more questions about Christianity and what it means, please write to me. I want to help you become all that God wants you to be. I also would be glad to send you more information about our Christian Athlete hockey camps, which provide opportunities for boys to learn more about Christ as well as to receive the best in hockey instruction from NHL players.

Please write me at this address:

Jean Pronovost
Hockey Ministries, International
P.O. Box 36
Beaconsfield, Quebec
Canada, H9W 5T6